# QUITTING MY FULL TIME JOB TO RAISE QUAILS

How I Made A Fortune And What You Can Learn From My Experience

Copyright © 2016 by Francis O. All rights reserved. The scanning, uploading, and distribution of this book via the internet or via any other means without the permission of the author is illegal and punishable by law. Please, purchase only authorized electronic editions, and do not participate in or encourage electronic piracy of copyrighted materials.

This book may not be re-sold or given away to other people. If you would like to share this book with another person, please purchase an additional copy for each recipient. If you're reading this book but did not purchase it or it was not purchased for your use only, kindly return it and purchase your own copy. Thank you for supporting the work of this author.

Although the author has made every effort to ensure the information herein was correct at the time of publication, the author does not assume and hereby disclaim any liability to any party for any loss, damage, or disruption caused by errors or omissions, whether such errors or omissions are from negligence, accident, or due to any other cause.

## Thank You

You could have picked hundreds of books to read, but you've settled on this one! Great Choice. I am glad you've picked it, and I hope it will be worth your time.

This is a short, yet comprehensive book on the subject of quail farming. I have carefully summarized all the vital points you need to know on successful quail farming.

There are endless books out there covering the same subject, but this one shares my personal experience, in a simple and straight forward manner. Herein, there are no sideshows or any unnecessary deviations into other subjects or topics. And the beauty of it all is that you can read this book from the front to the end in less than an hour!

**Dedication**

To those in pursuit of their dreams

# Contents

About this book..................................................7

How it all started.................................................9

My favorite quail breed and what you need to know about quail in general......................................................12

What it takes to raise quail: A quick A to Z guide................16

- Incubation..................................................16
- Feeding....................................................18
- Housing....................................................20
- Eggs: Laying and management................................22
- Health: Diseases and vices..................................24
- What you must do to raise strong, healthy, and productive quail........................................................28

How I earned a fortune from quail farming........................30

List of best performing quail breeds

- For egg production.........................................39
- For meat production........................................39

*To achieve the impossible, you must do the impossible. To achieve the ordinary, do the ordinary. To achieve nothing, do nothing! Always remember, the quality of your results will always depend on the quality of your input.*

**Anonymous**

# About This Book

*We no longer live in the land of surprises and unexpected miracles. Today, you must create your own surprises and miracles.*

Would you leave the comfort of a well-paying job to take a plunge in the unpredictable quail farming field?

Would you leave the comfort of a well-paying job to take a plunge in the unpredictable quail farming field? On the cold morning of Tuesday 13th February 2001, I made such uncomfortable decision that would later on turn my financial fortunes around!

What can you learn from my experience?

If you are interested in profitable quail farming as a beginner, you must read this book. Many people start quail farming without proper knowledge on how best to raise the birds, which best breeds to raise, and how to remain profitable in the venture. The beauty of this book lies in its simplicity, and in walking you through the vital steps, from start to finish. All important aspects quail farming has been carefully covered herein.

I know there are quite a number of books out there on quail farming, but this one is personalized to cover invaluable topics. It's my sincere belief the journey you are embarking on through reading this book to its end is one priceless investment you'll treasure forever!

# How It All Started

*What would you give up to succeed?*

On the chilly morning of Tuesday 13<sup>th</sup> February 2001, I made an uncomfortable decision to resign from my position of office administrator at a major construction company. I had worked there for close to ten years. And my major reason for resigning was due to love! Yes, I had fallen in deep love with quails. I had this undying urge to scale up my new found quail farming venture. This obsession just couldn't die away!

Before handing in my resignation letter, I first called my wife and broke to her the unexpected news.

'Hello dear'... I started the conversation with a weak and scared tone. I wasn't sure how Annette would react. We still had lots of pilling financial commitments that year to fulfill; two children in boarding school, a mortgage, and a car loan to cater for.

'Yes my dear', she warmly responded back. 'I hope all is well', she went on.

'Yes, all is well my dear'. I replied and proceeded. 'However, a new development has come up and I would love you being first person to hear it'.

'What is it my love?' She asked back, her voice now getting slightly shaky out of curiosity.

'Well, it's not all that good or bad news. It's something in-between. It's about a new adventure that I intend to pursue'. I went on.

And you can guess what transpired next!

Informing a stay-at-home wife that you are resigning from a well paying job to embark on raising quails is one of the most dreadful news you can ever break to an innocent soul! It's like stabbing that innocent soul with a crude and blunt weapon. But I had option. I had to do it since my vision and passion for raising the birds could not allow me to sit on that comfortable office chair any day longer.

Since childhood, I had always been fascinated by the idea of raising birds. One of my uncles, Dr. Meshack, owned an aviary housing several types of birds, and I would spend most of my childhood spare time helping him to feed the lovely creatures. I could watch birds like parakeets endlessly spilling feeds on the floor of the aviary, only for two bubbly Chinese painted quails to clean up the spilled feeds by feeding on them. That was the start of my love for quails.

As years passed by, I visited a total of fourteen quail farms, seven quail breeders, and eight suppliers of quail equipments. If I was to embark on keeping quails someday, like I knew I would eventually do, I had made a vow to learn all that was required towards raising the birds profitably. So when the time came for me to leave the comfort of that well-paying job, I had a rough idea of where I was headed to, and knew what was a waiting me. And yes, I ended up registering a huge success later on. Just read on.

In all honesty, there is no single day I do regret quitting my office job to keep the gorgeous birds!

# My Favorite Quail Breed And What You Need To Know About Quail In General

*To acquire knowledge, one must study; but to acquire wisdom, one must observe.*
Marilyn vos Savant

I made a firm decision to start the quail farming on a right foot. I did not want to take chances and gamble along the way. So I borrowed a sound advice from one experienced quail farmer and settled on one of the best performing quail breeds; the Jumbo Japanese quail. (Other good performing quail breeds you can consider raising are listed on page 39).

**Jumbo Japanese Quail**

The Jumbo Japanese quail is one of the best high performing mutants of the normal Japanese quail. They appear bigger in size when compared with the normal Japanese quail (mature jumbo Japanese quails grow to an average size of between 18-20cm, while mature normal Japanese quail grow to an average size of between 15-18cm.

Jumbo Japanese quail are great egg layers. With good care, they lay a minimum of 300 big-sized eggs per annum. And the beauty of their egg laying ability is that you can stimulate them into laying more through exposure to extended hours of lighting, giving them access to adequate clean and fresh water for drinking, and feeding them on well balanced and nutritious feeds rich in vitamins and proteins.

Jumbo Japanese quail are also great table birds. They mature fast, have excellent feed conversion ratio, and are favorably resistant to a number of poultry diseases.

Slightly away from my favorite quail breed, the Jumbo Japanese quail, here are some vital things you need to know about quail in general.

1. Quail are not poultry birds! Many people tend to suggest that quail are poultry birds. On the contrary, quail are game birds belonging to the same family as partridges and pheasants. This is vital to note since many quail farmers tend to feed the birds on commercial chicken feeds; without enriching the feeds with adequate proteins needed by quail.

2. Quail were originally domesticated for purposes of *cockfighting in Asia?* Interesting, fighting is one old habit that a number of male quails have found too hard to let go. If you raise mature male quail together in the same accommodation, they can easily pick a fight with each other. This is unlike female quails which have no urge to fight one another, not until provoked into fighting.

3. Due to their small-sized bodies, quail are at risk of being attacked by several predators including Dogs, Cats, Foxes, Rats, Skunks, Owls, Snakes Squirrels, Coyotes, Raccoons etc. You should therefore house them in the right structures and in the right locations.

4. Quail are more productive in a secure and peaceful environment. When stressed up, they tend to lose their productivity, thus raising them becoming unprofitable.

5. The quality and quantity of eggs you can get from quail is determined by the type of breed you are raising, the nature of care you are giving them, and the environment in which they are being raised.

6. Unlike hens, ducks, and other poultry breeds which are known to be noisy, quail are quiet birds; although certain breeds such as male Chicago quail are known to whistle, softly. In general, quail have a cool personality, making them great pets.

Today, domesticating quails is a growing trend among many households. This due to the birds' small sized bodies, making them ideal to be raised on small spaces - unlike other poultry breeds like chickens which require spacious structures for housing. If you have a small space within your backyard, or even a spare room indoors, you can comfortably raise a good number of quail.

# What It Takes To Raise Quail: A Quick A To Z Guide

*The larger the island of knowledge, the longer the shoreline of wonder*
**Ralph W. Sockman**

Before taking you through how I made a fortune from quail farming, let me first take you through what it takes, in general, to raise the birds. I will be taking you through incubation, all the way to things you must do to raise strong, healthy, and productive birds.

## Incubation

Most domesticated quails have no ability to go broody. They can't sit on their eggs and successfully hatch them. Subsequently, you can rely on a broody hen such as broody bantam, or use a manual/automatic egg incubator(s) to hatch their eggs.

On average, it takes 16 days for fertilized quail eggs to successfully hatch. However, there are other breeds whose fertilized eggs may take 17-19 days to hatch.

When relying on an artificial incubator to hatch quail eggs, you must carefully go through the manufacturer's manual on how to handle the machine, and how to maintain the required temperatures and humidity. Normally, the eggs require temperatures of $37^0$-$38^0$ celcius during incubation, with an average temperature of $37.5^0$ celcius being most ideal.

Place the eggs in the incubator with the pointed ends facing downwards, and turn them at least four times each 24 hours to guarantee uniform heating. Failure to do so may subject the eggs to overheating of one side and subsequently render them unable to hatch chicks.

Immediately you start incubating fertilized eggs, maintain humidity inside the incubator at (44-45)% until day 14 to 15. Once the eggshells start showing signs of cracking (piping - to allow the chicks out), stop turning the eggs and maintain the temperature at $37^0$ celcius. Once the chicks are fully out of the eggshells and have properly dried up, move them into a warm brooding area lit with a heating lump.

During their first week inside the brooder, maintain the temperatures at $34.5^0$-$35^0$ celcius. In the following weeks, reduce the temperatures by between 2-$3^0$ celcius each week until (5-6)[th] week when you should completely switch off the source of heat to enable the birds to fully adapt to the surrounding environment.

Quail chicks are generally very delicate to take care of. Did you know that drowning in drinking water is among the leading causes of mortality in quail chicks? Give them water in shallow dishes or put some pebbles or glass marbles in their drinkers to help minimize their chances of drowning in the water.

**Note:** When incubating fertilized quail eggs, you have no control of the sex of the birds that will come out of the eggs. You can get say, half females and half males, or more females than males, or more males than females.

**Feeding**

For the first two weeks, you can feed the chicks on a game bird starter mix. You can also give them a finely ground chick crumb starter. And when doing this, always remember that quail are game birds and not poultry. You should enrich any chicken or poultry related feeds you are giving them with adequate proteins.

**Purina game bird starter feed**

From there, upgrade their feeds to growers' until they reach six weeks old. Jumbo Japanese quail attain maturity at this stage and are usually ready to start laying eggs at six weeks.

For male birds (broilers) being raised for their meat, follow the growers' feeds with finishers' feeds. This is vital to help the birds gain good body weight and improve on the flavor of their meat. You can give them 45-50% corn alongside the finishers' feeds to not only help in improving the flavor of their meat, but to equally help in improving the succulence of their meat.

**One of the favorite layer's feeds in the United Kingdom**

For female birds (layers) being raised for eggs, follow the growers' feed with layers' pellets or layers' mash. This will help prepare their body for egg-laying and to improve on the flavor of their meat should they be slaughtered for their meat.

## Housing

At six weeks of age, transfer the quail from the brooder to a dry, secure and warm accommodation, free from exposure to disturbance, pests and predators.

Did you know a rabbit hutch with a run provides one of the best accommodations for quail? Other best alternatives for housing quail are cages or properly and securely constructed chicken coops. You can either construct quail's houses or purchase the houses from local dealers or suppliers.

The birds are generally unproductive in insecure and noisy environments. Therefore, shield them from predators such as cats, dogs, snakes, foxes etc. And as already stated, due their small-sized bodies, coupled with having a friendly personality, quail are usually easy targets for a host of predators.

Although the birds are known to be resistant to a number of poultry diseases, they sometimes can't survive in extreme temperatures. Therefore, during cold weather, heat their accommodation accordingly, or you can as well move them indoors while in their accommodation. You can also move them indoors during hot weather conditions, or insulate their accommodation against cold or hot temperatures.

Clean their accommodation regularly. Change their litter or bedding on a weekly basis to help curb build up of dirty litter which can easily aid spread of dirt-related infectious diseases such as Coccidiosis. Removing the dirty litter also shields the birds from attack by pests and parasites. Changing of worn out bedding and litter also prevents the birds from developing sores.

When quail are startled, they tend to shoot straight up just like a rocket. If their accommodation has a rough inside roofing i.e. weld-meshed roof or any other rough object, they can easily bang their heads hard on such objects, harming themselves in the process. Supplement the roofing of their accommodation with a secondary roof built of soft material such as a net to shield them from banging their heads when startled.

Quail have the ability to fly high and can easily disappear away if carelessly released in the open. You should therefore properly cover their coops or runs, and rightly clip their wings in case you intend to release them in any open environment.

Take lots of precaution when cleaning their cages or when changing their feeds and water. A single moment of lack of concentration can allow the birds to escape from their accommodation and fly away, never to return!

Provide the birds with adequate and appropriate low level perches. They will tend to playfully perch on them, exhibiting their natural behavior in the process.

**Eggs: Egg Laying and Management**

Quail begin laying eggs at the age of five, six or seven weeks

(depending on the breed you are raising) and reaches full egg production at 50-60 days later.

Jumbo Japanese quails lay at least 300 eggs per annum, when properly taken good care of. Interestingly, they sometimes lay twice a day, especially during summer. To stimulate the birds to lay more eggs, provide them with correct feeds rich in protein, and expose them to at least 14-16 hours of light each 24 hours. However you need to take note that all egg laying birds have a limited egg laying potential. Stimulating the birds to start laying many eggs consistently in the early years may subject them egg-dropping sooner. If you stimulate the hens to start laying many eggs in their first year of egg laying, they may end up dropping their ability to lay the many eggs as early as the second year.

Female Jumbo Japanese quail often start laying eggs at six weeks of age. Immediately they begin laying eggs, desist from the urge of wanting to stimulate them into laying many eggs immediately. This can be detrimental to their long term health and productivity. At that age, their body frame isn't fully developed and adapted into laying many eggs. Start them off with natural light and adjust the lighting later on as the birds mature up and gets into the right body frame.

Many female quail prefer laying eggs in the afternoons or in the evenings. Their egg laying ability then tend to drop off in the second year (when using artificial light), and in the 2.5 or $3^{rd}$ year (when relying on natural light).

## Collecting Eggs

Before collecting quail eggs, wash your hands properly and dry them with a clean towel. Ensure your hands are free from dirt.

Collect the eggs twice a day and store them in a clean room with temperatures between $12°c$ to $14°c$ - ideally, store the eggs at room temperature.

## Health: Diseases and Vices

To raise healthy and productive quail, they require well balanced and nutritious feeds, clean water, warm, dry and secure housing, and most importantly, timely attention. This can never be overemphasized.

When quail tend to exhibit lethargy, abnormally colored droppings, sudden discharge from beak, and poor appetite, immediately, isolate such bird from the rest of the flock. This is vital to help curb spread that infection to other birds, and to give the affected bird an ample opportunity to be monitored and recover.

Did you know inactive birds can easily catch the attention of vibrant birds within the flock. Consequently, the inactive birds can easily fall victims of bullying or pecking by the aggressive birds?

Did you know quail diseases caused by bacterial infection can easily be treated with antibiotics, while those caused by virus are hard to treat and may be fatal to the affected birds? Closely monitor the birds to put under control any disease infection within the flock.

Quail are susceptible to infection by certain bacterial diseases affecting their respiratory tracts. Such infections include: pneumonia, bronchitis, infectious sinusitis and chronic respiratory disease. These infections are largely characterized by loss of appetite, nasal discharge, and difficulty in breathing.

## Coccidiosis

One of the most common bacterial digestive infections affecting quail is Coccidiosis. Birds infected with coccidiosis exhibit an unusual greenish dropping of a more slimy nature. To contain coccidiosis, exercise good hygiene and consult a trained and experienced vet on the best antibiotic to use. You can also give the birds, especially quail chicks, starters laced with coccidiostat. It's one of the effective ways of containing infection of this sometimes fatal quail disease.

## Enteritis

Birds suffering from this infection tend to exhibit symptoms similar to those of coccidiosis, such as an unusual greenish dropping. To contain it, exercise good hygiene standard when handling the birds and consult a trained vet on which best drug to administer.

## Salmonella/Worms

This is one of the most lethal quail infections. Birds infected with worms may register increased appetite but reduced body weight, and may also be having pieces of the worms attached to their excretions. To contain worm infection, keep the feeders and drinkers properly disinfected and regularly cleaned. Give the birds clean water all the time and ensure their feeds are clean as well. Summarily, ensure you raise the birds under good hygienic standards and occasional consult a trained vet on best drugs to administer to deworm the birds.

**Vices**

Vices are bad habits that quail develop due to their environmental exposure. The three most common quail vices are:
- *Feather and vent pecking,*
- *Egg pecking,*
- *Cannibalism.*

**Causes of Vices and Management**

Quail may develop vices due to a number of reasons including: lack of necessary minerals such as calcium and phosphorus in their feeds, idleness, prolonged exposure to laid eggs, prolonged exposure to broken or soft-shelled eggs, overcrowding in the birds' accommodation, introduction of new birds with bad habits into an old flock with good habits, attack by pets and parasites, and mixing of younger birds with older birds in the same accommodation make the younger birds be susceptible to bullying (pecking) by the older birds.

Below are some simple, yet effective measures you can take to help tame vices in quail:

- ✓ Give the birds well-balanced and nutritious feeds containing all the necessary nutrients and minerals they need in adequate quantity.

- ✓ Raise the correct number of birds per coop and keep them busy throughout the day. You can hang some green vegetables within their accommodation to keep them busy. An idle bird is susceptible to developing pecking and cannibalism traits.

✓ To avoid exposing the birds to laid eggs for a prolonged time, collect the eggs in a timely manner from the laying nests; two to three times each day.

✓ Identify, cull and de-beak any noted egg-eating or cannibal within the flock.

✓ Keep younger birds separate from older birds to help shield the younger birds from bullying by the older aggressive birds.

✓ Dust the birds regularly with correct pesticides to contain attack and spread of pests and parasites.

✓ Identify and separate from the rest of the flock any bird which is prone to regular pecking by others, or that which is aggressively attacking others. This will help tame pecking and cannibalism within the flock.

# What You Must Do To Raise Strong, Healthy, And Productive Quail

To raise strong, healthy and productive quail, exercise the below:

Feed the birds on adequate, well-balanced and nutritious feeds containing all the necessary nutrients and minerals they need.

Give the birds clean and fresh water for drinking. The water should be placed in secure drinkers and at convenient locations where the birds do not need to strain to access them. Equally, ensure the feeders and waterers are adequate in number to prevent the birds from fighting over them.

Keep the birds in an appropriate accommodation, free from noise and intruders. Such environment helps in keeping quail calm and active, thus boosting their productivity.

Give the birds adequate perches to enable them feel at home (to enable them exhibit their natural behavior within their accommodations).

Keep the correct number of quail per housing. Overcrowding the birds in a single house can stress them and force them to start fighting each other for space, feeds and water.

Examine the birds after every three to four weeks for mites, ticks and lice. If positive, dust them appropriately with louse powder or redmite powder. Get a good recommendation from a trained vet on which drug to use. In fact, before you embark on keeping quail, ensure you have details of a trained and experienced vet who you can rely on.

Clean the birds' accommodation regularly off droppings and provide them with clean friendly bedding and points for sand bathing. Keep their accommodation clean, dry, secure and warm at all times.

In a nutshell, to raise strong, healthy and productive birds, you must give the birds the right care, the right feeds, raise them in an appropriate accommodation, and ensure they are clean and disease free

# How I Earned A Fortune From Quail Farming

*There is never an appropriate time to start any successful venture. You simply must trust your gut feeling, go out there and put your best foot forward. Remember, fortune favors the brave.*

When I started raising quail, a number of close friends and relatives could not clearly fathom why I was leaving a well-paying job for the awkward quail farming venture. In fact, a number of them openly advised me to think otherwise; to raise the birds only as a hobby. But shock on them, I had already made up my mind! I was psychologically prepared for what was to come my way, success or failure. If I was to fail, I had something to learn, and if I was to succeed, I had everything to carry home. Anyway, you'll never know how strong you are until being strong is your only option!

Back then, quail farming wasn't as flooded as it is today. There were just a bunch of few farmers whose who were raising the birds for egg and meat production for domestic consumption.

However, it was during that time when the number of people interested in commercial quail farming started to grow. There was already a growing ready market for quail products. Interestingly, the demand for these products started to outdo the production capacity of the fewer quail farmers.

If I was to make my kill, I had to come up with a unique strategy that would give me an edge over the competition. Given that I had spent many years with a number of local quail farmers, breeders and suppliers of quail products, I already had had an ample opportunity to carry out relevant research on which quail products to focus on. Specifically, I planned on developing a one stop farm for anyone who wanted anything related to quail.

I started off by raising 400 female Jumbo Japanese quail together with 200 male Jumbo Japanese quail. I started by raising the birds for producing fertilized eggs. Surprisingly, three months into the venture, I started getting unending orders for unfertilized eggs from a sharply growing list of clients. The demand for those unfertilized eggs ended up outperforming the demand for fertilized eggs, given that my Jumbo Japanese quail were laying slightly bigger eggs than those of other local quail farmers (most of them kept the normal Japanese quail).

Without wasting time, I tripled the number of female Jumbo Japanese quail I was raising to meet the increased demand for the unfertilized eggs. I raised the new birds I brought in separate from the old flock, and away from the males. Two weeks later, the birds began laying eggs (I had brought in birds which were at the point of lay).

As time progressed, I started receiving orders from new farmers in need of quail chicks and point of lay birds. Given that I wasn't hatching fertilized eggs by then, I had to act fast and grab that opportunity of hatching fertilized eggs. Using the money secured from egg sales together with part of my savings, I placed an order for an artificial incubator capable of hatching 2000 eggs. I wanted to embark on hatching the chicks on a large scale and sell them at favorable prices. This was the only way to catch up with the local breeders and other quail farmers who had started hatching fertilized eggs and were selling at unfavorable prices. After all, there was a ready market.

One Thursday evening as I was seated at home waiting for the arrival of the incubator, I got this shocking call from a strange number informing me that he was involved in a grisly road accident, and that the incubator he was transporting to my farm was damaged beyond repair!

'Sometimes some people say strange things!' I inwardly wondered in shock as I ended the conversation. I remember paying the full cost of the machine together with the cost of transport, only to be informed that the incubator was no more!

Well, desperate times call for desperate measures. Although I got an assurance that the insurance company would fully pay for the damages, I was informed by the vehicles' owner that the process would take close to a year before being fully finalized.

I wasn't ready to wait for a week, a month, forget about a year, to start hatching the eggs. So in a desperate move, I went to a very close and trusted friend and borrowed money. Truth is, I did not want to take a loan from my bank since the financial institution was charging an exorbitant interest rate on the amount I was after.

After securing the credit, I went ahead and bought an incubator with the same capacity to hold 2000 eggs. And this time round, I did not wait for the machine to be transported to my farm at a later a date, I insisted on it being delivered to my farm on the same day of purchase. And yes, it arrived without a hitch.

Given that my hens could not lay enough eggs to fill up the incubator, I contracted a few select local farmers who were keeping Jumbo Japanese quail to bridge the deficit. And within six weeks, believe you me, the demand for quail chicks from my farm ended up outrunning my production capacity.

One year and half later, I noted something strange. When I started incubating the eggs, I used to enjoy a 90% hatch rate. But this enviable rate dropped to 70%. Something odd was seriously going on and it was time to establish it and put an end to it, else I was going to be forced to close shop, sooner than later.

Upon proper investigation, I unraveled that a number of quail farmers I had trusted to supply my farm with fertilized eggs took advantage of my confidence in them and started supplying my farm with all manner of eggs; unfertilized eggs, eggs from older breeds of quail, and eggs which had taken too long after being laid. Equally, I realized that the incubator I was using wasn't correctly functioning. It could not consistently maintain the required temperatures and humidity during incubation. Remember that for an incubator to successfully hatch quail eggs it has provide three vital things: suitable temperature, relative humidity, and adequate fresh air.

To turn my fortunes around, I took the painful decision of cutting off links with the rogue and ungrateful suppliers, and decided to start incubating eggs from my farm. Equally, I went ahead and brought in an experienced technician who helped in servicing the incubator from time to time.

To hasten my production capacity of fertilized eggs, I bought more Jumbo Japanese quails; hens which were at the point of lay and mature males. I then housed them in a ratio of two hens to one male. This was vital to ensure the eggs I was going to get from the birds were fertile.

Significantly, incubating eggs from my own farm gave me an enviable opportunity to incubate truly fertilized eggs, clean eggs, eggs from young but mature hens, and eggs which have not taken too long after being laid.

Within three months, the eggs from my farm were able to start filling up the incubator. Notably, I was now purchasing fertilized eggs from my own farm, incubating them, and later on, selling the hatched chicks at favorable prices.

To derive some favorable profit, I ensured the average cost of each quail chick was slightly above the average cost of each fertilized egg, together with the cost of running the incubator.

Six months later, I was able to secure orders for all hatched quail chicks. Consequently, I was able to pay back the amount I had borrowed. I ended up giving him some extra payment as a way of thanking him.

To give my competition a run for their money, I decided to reduce my prices. I started selling at between $1 and $1.5 below their prices. Given that I was no longer relying on other farmers for fertilized eggs, I was able to enjoy high turnovers, whilst effectively managing my costs. This ensured I enjoyed some good profit margins.

I would later on continue receiving unending orders for fertilized. This prompted me to triple the numbers of birds I was raising to get enough eggs for incubation and surplus ones to sell to other farmers, breeders, food outlets, groceries, supermarkets, and other walk-in buyers.

Later on, as my farm expanded with various aspects of quail products, I started receiving inquiries from farmers and local institutions who wanted to learn a thing or two about quail farming. Fast on my feet, I embraced the idea and started charging them a fee when visiting my farm, and for sparing my time to give them tips on quail farming and information related to quail.

In a nutshell, below is a quick summary of how I earned a fortune from quail farming. The figures below are an accumulation of what I earned within a period of two years and ten months - between February 2001 to end of December 2003.

Let the figures do the talking now

1. **Consultation fees:** I levied consultation fees on people who were in need of my professional advice on various aspects of quail farming. I used to charge between $15-$30 per session of not more than three hours. This earned me a total of $35,000 within the period of two years and ten months.

2. **Farm entrance fees**: I levied farm entrance fees for those who visited my farm to learn/see how I was raising the birds. This was vital to ensure that I could raise enough money to purchase nutritious feeds for the birds to compensate them for withstanding presence of endless number of strangers within their sight. I levied between $2 and $5 per person. Within the period of two years and ten months, this earned me a total of $26,000.

3. **Selling of both fertilized and unfertilized eggs:** I was selling both fertilized and unfertilized eggs. I had an endless list of clients since many people loved the products from my farm. I focused on giving all my clients value for their money. I was primarily selling to other

quail farmers, breeders, food outlets, groceries, supermarkets, and walk-in buyers. The sale of quail eggs earned me a total of $55,000.

4. **Selling of quail chicks:** I was selling day old and up to point of lay hens. Equally, I was selling day old and up to 3-5 weeks old broilers. In two years and ten months, this earned me a total of $48,000.

5. **Selling of meat birds:** I was selling meat birds; mature broilers, and mature hens past egg-laying (hens that had stopped laying eggs). This earned me a total of $35,000 within the two years and ten months.

6. **Quail manure:** I was selling quail manure to local farmers who were growing horticultural crops. Within the two years and ten months, this earned me a total of $10,400.

7. **Selling/referring of quail drugs:** I used to sell certain quail drugs to fellow farmers at a commission. I was also earning a commission for referring sellers of quail drugs to a number of local quail farmers who sought my help. This earned me a total of $29,500 within the two years and ten months.

8. **Selling of quail equipments.** I was also being paid a commission by some manufacturers of quail farming equipments for selling their equipments such as drinkers, waterers, cages, rodent stoppers etc to fellow quail farmers, and by referring quail farmers in need of them.

Within two years and ten months, this earned me a whopping $33,000.

You can do the mathematics. Before starting quail farming, I was on a contract earning me an annual gross income of $55,000. But when you do the calculations of the gross amount I earned from my farm within two years and ten months, you will approve it was worth the risk.

And it didn't end there! I later on received another incubator from the insurance company. This propelled my farm into massive operations. In fact, many local commercial quail farmers were forced to close shop since they could not match my operations.

And yes, I am still raising quail to date, though I have equally diversified into real estate to broaden my income net. And as a parting shot, the best advice I can freely give to anyone interested in starting quail farming, or any other business venture is, *'there is never an appropriate time to start any successful venture. You simply must trust your gut feeling, go out there and put your best foot forward. You'll never know how much you can achieve until you try.*

# List of Best Performing Quail Breeds

Below is a small list of some of the best performing quail breeds you can consider raising for commercial or domestic production of eggs and meat.

**For egg production**

- Jumbo Japanese
- Tuxedo
- Manchurian Golden
- English White
- British Range
- Normal Japanese

**For meat production**

- Normal Japanese
- Jumbo Japanese
- Bob White (American)
- White Breasted Indian
- The King Quail/Chinese Painted Quail ( this is also a good aviary bird)

*Thanks for reading and good luck!*

www.ingramcontent.com/pod-product-compliance
Lightning Source LLC
Chambersburg PA
CBHW070420190526
45169CB00003B/1337